# ACT IN THE TREATMENT OF OBSESSIONS OF A SEXUAL NATURE



ISBN: 9798882921841

## THANKS

These lines will serve as thanks to all those people who in one way or another have helped to make this work.

## INDEX

## GENERAL INTRODUCTION

Clinical psychologists rarely meet clients who seek help for obsessions of a sexual nature. However, this may not be due to the fact that this problem is infrequent but rather to the modesty of the people when dealing with these issues. In any case, as professional you must be prepared to deal with cases of this type, even if they are few, at the time they are presented in your consultation. This book, analyzing three clinical cases, aims to shed some light when it comes to treating cases related to obsessions of a sexual nature. These three cases have been treated through Acceptance and Commitment Therapy or ACT (Hayes, Strosahl y Wilson, 1999). This form of therapy, with the theoretical support of Relational Frame Theory (Hayes, Barnes-Holmes y Roche, 2001), treats the behavioral problems of patients, emphasizing the analysis of the role that the experiential avoidance of private events plays in the genesis and maintenance of a multitude of problems of a psychological nature and offering a series of useful therapeutic tools to change these avoidant and dysfunctional patterns.

These clinical cases, before being treated by ACT, are analyzed from the perspective of the theoretical approach of the Model of Tension Mechanisms proposed in the book *Uncontrollable Thoughts: The Model of Tension Mechanisms in Human Psychopathology* (Jiménez, 2012) based on the Experiential Avoidance Disorder (Hayes, Wilson, Gifford, Follette y Stroshal, 1996) and the Theory of Behavior Completion Mechanisms (McConaghy, 1980).

The Experiential Avoidance Disorder (Hayes et al., 1996) refers to a functional dimension of psychological suffering in which an individual is chronically and persistently involved, despite how maladaptive this is for his life. Basically, what its advocates propose is that a person's efforts to avoid certain thoughts, feelings, physiological sensations, or private events of any kind, produce the opposite effect. In this way, when a person, motivated by various circumstances present in their personal learning context or history, says to themselves: «I have to avoid thinking that *I am a strange or abnormal person*», that verbal statement contains the avoided content «*I am a strange or abnormal person soy una person*», producing a paradoxical effect.

The Model of Tension Mechanisms assumes the paradoxical phenomena of Experiential Avoidance Disorder (Hayes et al., 1996) and gives a determining role to tension, understood as physiological discomfort or unpleasant physiological activation, in the functional explanation of many psychological disorders. This last postulate is developed directly from the Theory of Behavior Completion Mechanisms (McConaghy, 1980), which argues that when a person is faced with a stimulating situation classified as threatening, an aversive physiological activation occurs that only disappears by carrying out a compulsive contact or approach behavior towards that stimulus. This phenomenon would follow a pattern of negative reinforcement in which the reinforcement of the behavior would be the elimination of feelings of discomfort and anxiety.

Combining the Experiential Avoidance Disorder (Hayes et al., 1996) and Theory of Behavior Completion Mechanisms (McConaghy, 1980), is possible understood how the sexual concerns and obsessions present in the clinical cases analyzed in this book can be established chronically and how, to reduce the tension associated with all these aversive events (which paradoxically increase when trying to be avoided), maladaptive or problematic behaviors can be carried out.

Throughout this book, we will see how ACT is a useful therapeutic tool to unmask and disarm the processes described above, taking the protagonists of each clinical case out of the vicious, apparently dead-end, circles in which they have been involved.

## References

Hayes, S.C., Wilson, K.G., Gifford, E.V., Follete, V.M. y Strosahl, K. (1996). Experiential avoidance and behavior disorder: a functional dimensional approach to diagnoses and treatment. *Journal of Consulting and Clinical Psychology, 64*, 1.152-1.168.

Hayes, S.C., Strosahl, K.D. y Wilson, K.G. (1999) *Accepttance and conmmitment therapy. An experiential approach to behavior change.* NuevaYork: Guilford Press.

Jiménez, R. (2012). *Pensamientos Incontrolables: El Modelo de los Mecanismos Tensionales en la Psicopatología Humana.* Raleigh: Lulu Press.

Jiménez, R. (2014). *Terapia de Aceptación y Compromiso: Abordaje de cinco casos clínicos.* Raleigh: Lulu Press.

McConaghy, N. (1980). *Behavior Completion Mechanisms.* New York: Plenum Press.

## CLINICAL CASE 1

### Description of the clinical case

The client in the clinical case presented below is Sandra, a 21 year old woman, a university law student who asked for help in anguish because she had serious doubts about her sexual orientation. She had not attended college classes for several weeks, according to her because her obsessions did not allow her to concentrate, and she had also reduced her social events such as attending parties or meetings with friends.

The client narrated her story since she was a little girl, saying that she was the only girl of the family and that she had three older brothers, all boys. Sandra related that she spent a lot of time with them and enjoyed playing games that, at that time, were considered typically masculine such as soccer, «cops and robbers», «cowboys» or «gladiatorial fights». She remember that her parents frequently berated her for playing boy games, warning her that she would turn into a tomboy.

On the other hand, Sandra remembered that since she was little she was good at sports, she was a fast and energetic girl and, therefore, received a lot of ridicule from her classmates. They frequently criticized her and even insulted her, which affected Sandra a lot and made it difficult for her to interact with other girls at her school. During adolescence, Sandra was a shy, insecure and introverted girl.

Besides, although the client initially reported experiencing some sexual attraction to boys, she often found herself looking at other girls. Apparently, she did it to compare herself with them, since Sandra was a slip, athletic and a little gangly girl who, unlike most of her classmates, took time to develop her breasts.

Sandra reported that, as time went by, she began to worry about the possibility that this initial admiration or envy could lead to some type of sexual attraction towards girls. At this point, the client felt a strong need to make sure that she was not attracted to women, only men. So, when she came across an attractive girl, she would look at her to make sure she was not attracted to any kind of attraction. The fact that she was constantly looking at other girls (although initially the reason for doing so was to see if they attracted him or not), as well as being able to really appreciate the physical attractiveness in women, was causing Sandra a lot of concern. The client thought that if she looked at them so frequently and was able to appreciate their attractiveness it was because perhaps she was a lesbian. This idea terrified Sandra who said to herself: «I have to avoid thinking that I am a lesbian» or «I have to stop thinking about other women». Sandra reports that the more she tried to avoid these types of thoughts, paradoxically, the more insidious they became.

On the other hand, the client reported that since she was approximately 15 years old she had been masturbating thinking about boys and trying not to let images of women cross her mind. She said that to herself: «Try not to think about women» and, paradoxically, images of women appeared in his mind. In addition, Sandra commented that without understanding the reason very well, these images were accompanied by a certain pleasant relaxation and groinal response, which caused her great anguish. Sandra would then try to make sure that these mental images were not pleasant for her by briefly fantasizing about them to see what effect they had on her. Unfortunately, she discovered that this approach to the images that she tried to avoid did result in a certain way pleasurable for her. As the result of her survey was not what she expected, Sandra felt increasingly confused and guilty.

This vicious circle was repeated on multiple occasions following the same script. Upon reaching adulthood, with many doubts and insecurities about herself and her sexuality, Sandra began to worry that she might be able to move from fantasy to reality. In addition, Sandra stated that she experienced some difficulties in interacting sexually with boys, since according to her physique was not very attractive and she was shy and insecure. Despite these difficulties, her first sexual relationships were with men, but these relationships were not entirely satisfactory for her, since she experienced them as a kind of test or exam in which she forced herself to enjoy herself to make sure that she really was not lesbian. With this self-applied pressure, the fact that she did not fully enjoy with men was an indication to the client of her possible lesbianism.

## Functional analysis of the case

Analyzing all the information provided by the client Sandra, it seems clear that we are dealing with a case of what was formerly known as «egodystonic homosexuality» or, as it is currently called «internalized homophobia». However, from an approach based on functional analysis, it should be made clear that this diagnostic name has limited practical use, since it does not offer any key at a functional level that can guide us when planning a clinical intervention. In order to establish the appropriate treatment, it is essential to carry out a functional analysis of problem behaviors with the aim of acting on the relevant variables of this specific case.

The answers that the client Sandra indicates as problematic are the recurrent sexual thoughts about women and the concern about the possibility of carrying out sexual contacts with people of their own sex in reality. From a topographical point of view, we can consider that the obsessions related to homosexuality that occur when the client is about to masturbate (stimulating trigger situation), are preceded by the following responses:

1) Previous verbal-cognitive response: the client has thoughts of the type «I'm sure I'll think of the same thing again», «I have to avoid thinking about

women», «I have to control this», «These thoughts give me pleasure, maybe I like women» and «I am abnormal for thinking these things».

2) Previous physiological response: The cognitive or verbal responses indicated in the previous point are accompanied by an unpleasant physiological activation (tension, agitation, anxiety, etc.) and some pre-sexual activation (lubrication of the vagina).

As can be seen, the verbal responses related to fear, avoidance and guilt are accompanied by physiological activation that the client experiences as aversive. In addition, this unpleasant physiological activation is joined by a certain sexual activation (despite being classified as immoral and inappropriate by the client).

On the other hand, avoidant thoughts paradoxically make the contents that are entended to be avoided even more present in the client. When any person tries to avoid or delete content X, they will necessarily be in relation or in contact with said content X, producing a paradoxical effect. In our case, when Sandra says to herself «I have to avoid thinking about *women*», that statement already contains the avoided content «*women*». The client experiences some instantaneous relaxation just as that avoided content «*women*» appears in her mind, since if the content she was worried about appearing has already appeared in her mind, she saves herself some of the effort needed to keep repressing or suppressing that content.

This small fortuitous relaxation coupled with the perception of her own pre-sexual arousal makes the client feel even more guilty, as she values these experience as physically pleasurable despite the fact that they do not seem. morally acceptable to her. In addition, these insights focus her on anticipating the future pleasure she may experience if she voluntarily accepts those thoughts or mental images, rather than trying to suppress them. Therefore, the client decides to carry out small «experiments» or verification probes, briefly fantasizing about those thoughts or mental images, to see if they really are pleasant or not. Indeed, when the client allows such mental content to emerge, she experiences pleasure in discharging unpleasant physiological arousal caused by efforts at repression. As the results of her probes are not what she wanted, the client feels increasingly confused and guilty.

The client experienced great physiological tension when she tried to control or avoid her thoughts and all efforts to avoid these sensations were unsuccessful and paradoxically made her feel worse and worse. She already knew that if she masturbated by allowing these fantasies, then she would end up feeling bad and guilty about herself, but the point is that she was already feeling bad befote doing it. Furthermore, due to the paradoxical effects of experiential avoidance described above, there was no effective way to suppress Duch mental content.

At a topographical level, the answers that Sandra emits when she surrenders and masturbates, allowing homosexual fantasies, are the following:

1) Verbal-cognitive response: The client, alter struggling unsuccessfully to control and try to eliminate sexual content related to women from her mind, has the following thought: «I can't stand this anguish, I give up».

2) Locomotor response: The client ends up masturbating.

3) Physiological response: Sudden, pleasurable discharge from previous physiological arousal.

As we can see, the client's behaviour would follow a pattern of negative reinforcement (the client manages to eliminate physiological discomfort). The consequences of the responses she emits are clear, in the short term the client has discharged the physiological discomfort triggered by the attempts to avoid/control the problem behavior, but in the long term, negative consequences continue to be triggered (increased guilt, increased moral conflict when associating pleasure with homosexual stimuli, deterioration of self-esteem, etc.). These negative consequences will predispose the client to try harder to control her thoughts and feelings the next time she is faced with the possibility of masturbating to homosexual fantasies or the possibility of actual homosexual contact.

## Therapeutic treatment of the clinical case based on Acceptance and Commitment Therapy

Taking into account the previous functional and topographical analysis, the clinical intervention was aimed at making the client reconsider the functionality of her control/avoidance behavior of thoughts and sensations, given that the control/avoidance attempt itself was the main factor in her psychological problem.

The first step was to encourage «creative despair» (Wilson y Luciano, 2002) so that the client became aware that, despite all her efforts to control or avoid the thoughts or sensations that tormented her, she had not achieved any positive results. To facilitate this process, the «metaphor of the hole» (Wilson y Luciano, 2002) was used. By way of summary, this metaphor exposes the situation of a man who tries to get out of the hole in which he is trapped by digging with a shovel. The result is that the hole gets deeper and deeper and the man sinks deeper and deeper.

Despite the fact that Sandra understood relatively well that the attempts to suppress the thoughts that she feared increased her physiological activation, she was very resistant to remaining passive before them, because she was convinced that it was her obligation to suppress them. In this way, enough emphasis had to be placed for the client to assimilate that the therapeutic acceptance of the thoughts that were proposed to her did not imply agreeing with their content. To do this, the process known as «separation of the context self and the content self» was sought, through the use of various metaphors, including the metaphor of «the apartment building and the neighbors». According to this metaphor, the apartment building would be equivalent to the self as context while the different neighbors who inhabit it would refer to the self as content. The qualities attributed to each of the neighbors (good, bad, pleasant, unpleasant, etc.) do not have to be generalized to the building itself.

In addition to the use of therapeutic metaphors, the client was explained how, regardless of the sexual orientation of each one, it is normal for all people to occasionally have sexual thoughts of diverse content and that this does not imply that the person necessarily agree with said content, much less want to put the situations they represent into practice in real life.

This approach, although in session it was comforting for the client, did not produce the desired cognitive defusion. It did not help Sandra to learn to «detach» herself from her private events. For this reason, the matter continued to be worked on in subsequent through the use of various metaphors, including the one that appears in Hayes' book «Get out of your mind and into your life», known as «the train of the mind». The client was asked to imagine she was on a bridge over a train track and watch three trains pass under the bridge. One of the trains was loaded with sensations-emotions, another with thoughts-appraisals, and the third with impulses and tendencies. Subsequently, she was asked to think about her own sensations-emotions, thoughts-appraisals or impulses-tendencies. When Sandra was merged with her private events and fell into experiential avoidance, it's like she was riding on one of the trains. To finish, she is asked to visualize herself as a spectator watching the trains go by from the top of the bridge and, in this situation, perceive the difference between riding the trains and watching the trains go by.

Despite the fact that with the passing of the sessions, Sandra was learning better and better to detach herself and distance herself from her private events, there was a factor that continued to lead her to try to keep homosexual thoughts and images under control. Apart from the fact that she considered certain mental contents immoral, the fear of being able to go from fantasy to reality led her to revert to patterns of control and avoidance. In this regard, it was explained to him that no matter how much he tried, there would always be the real possibility of committing the acts he feared. Theoretically, there would always be a possibility, however remote. No matter how hard she tried to make sure, she could never be 100 percent sure, and she would have to tolerate uncertainty. Although this approach initially caused the client great anxiety, several work sessions were carried out in exposure to these thoughts through the experiential exposure exercise that appears in the manual by Wilson and Luciano (2002).

Finally, Sandra made a commitment to accept that these thoughts and worries would continue to appear, but this would not prevent her from leading a fulfilling, goal-oriented life, according to her values. In relation to this, the client established the following values:

-Be a good lawyer
-Be a hardworking person
-Be a living person

At this point in therapy, the theme of commitment was emphasized by asking: «Are you willing to accept all your inner experiences, no matter how painful they may be, if this is necessary to live a worthwhile life?», making it clear that there were only two possible answers: yes or no. Sandra could not commit halfway and had to be clear that the commitment process is a dynamic factor. For this reason, it was explained to him that committing, from the meaning that it takes in ACT, is not signing a kind of contract before a notary that guarantees for life that one will always be able to carry out the acceptance and defusion keys worked on throughout of therapy. Sandra should ask herself the question: «¿Are you willing to accept all your inner experiences, no matter how painful they may be, if it is necessary to live a valuable life?» over and over again throughout his life.

Before finishing the intervention with Sandra, several sessions were dedicated to training in social skills using the modelling and role-playing technique with the aim of improving the young woman's repertoire of communicative behaviours to help her relate better with men, with who showed some difficulty in communicating, given his shyness.

In total, 16 weekly sessions were carried out, of which the first two were for evaluation and presentation of the singularities of ACT to the client and 12 sessions were for treatment itself.

Two months later, Sandra was contacted by telephone to monitor her therapeutic evolution. Sandra reported that although she still had female-related thoughts and images, these were less intense, were not accompained by as unpleasant physiological arousal as she had experienced in the past, and were usually replaced without too much difficulty by fantasies related to men. Six months later, the last telephone contact with Sandra was carried out and her positive evolution was confirmed, since, according to the client, sexual thoughts related to women hardly appeared and, when they did, they did not disturb her too much, even if they appeared during masturbation, in phases of maximun excitement. In relation to her values, the client had taken up law classes again, had gotten a job as a clerk in a clothing store and, although at the moment she had not been able to start any heterosexual sentimental relationship, she stated that she had met quite a few boys and felt less shy and much safer and more comfortable when interacting socially with them.

## CLINICAL CASE 2

### Description of the clinical case

The client of the clinical case that is presented below is Rodrigo, a 27 year old man, single and with a job as a security guard in a shopping center. Rodrigo requested help to try to control some obsessive thoughts of a sexual nature, which he had been suffering from for several years.

The client mentioned that since he was a child he was a little shy, insecure and somewhat fearful, influenced by overprotective parents and by the fact that he grew up in a rural area, without contact with many children his age, except during school hours where he went, located in a town about 10 kilometers from his home. Rodrigo had no contact with his classmates once school hours were over. For this reason, Rodrigo believes that he grew up as a shy child with few social skills. He had difficulty making friends and felt insecure and low on self-esteem. The client reports that, when he was 10 years old, he began to experience attraction to girls his age. Rodrigo reported that he masturbated thinking about them, but was never able to interact socially with any of them. A couple of years later, some of his classmates were already dating girls and recounting their first sexual flings with them and, for this reason, Rodrigo assures that he felt inferior and self-conscious about them. The client thought at that time that he would never have a girlfriend or be with any girl due to his shyness and feared that his only sexual experience would be masturbation.

It is in this context, with these predisposing factors, when an event occurs that would end up becoming the main precipitating factor of the problems for which Rodrigo requested therapeutic help. When the client was 15 years old, he was left in the care of several ponies (dwarf horses) owned by his father. His parents had gone to town to shop at the supermarket and he was left in charge. At this point in the story, Rodrigo verbalizes that he suddenly stared at the genitals of one of the female ponies and was amazed at how similar they were to those of the naked women he had seen, a few months earlier, in a pornographic magazine he had published one of the classmates had shown him at recess. With astonishment, he verified that he had an erection at that moment and the possibility of penetrating the animal flashed through his mind. He tried to put that idea out of his mind, considering it immoral, but at the same time he was very sexually curious. Rodrigo assures that he even took off his pants and went towards the pony, but when she noticed the boy's movements she moved a few steps away. At that moment, always according to the version given by the client himself, Rodrigo froze, regretted carrying out his idea and pulled up his pants.

Although finally Rodrigo had discarded the idea, overcoming the temptation, he felt very guilty for having considered such a possibility. As a result of that episode, Rodrigo began to make an effort not to have sexual thoughts when he was in situations where he was alone with the family animals.

Rodrigo, who used to masturbate daily, quickly became concerned that his sexual fantasies might include images of the female pony he was about to penetrate. According to him, he gave himself instructions such as: «I'm not going to think about having sex with animals», but, paradoxically, he ended up thinking about it. Rodrigo mentions that, without really understanding the reason, when these thoughts that he was trying to repress ended up appearing, they did so accompanied by a certain pleasant relaxation, a fact that greatly distressed him. In addition, Rodrigo mentions that he noticed a certain groinal response under the influence of these thoughts. The client experienced a kind of anticipation of pleasure when in contact with these images. Then, Rodrigo tried to make absolutely sure that those thoughts were not pleasant for him, briefly fantasizing about them to see what effect they had on him. Much to his chagrin, he discovered that this approach to the thoughts he was trying to avoid was actually pleasurable for him. Because the result of his probing was not what he expected, but he had actually experienced pleasure in fantasizing the thoughts he was trying to repress, the client felt increasingly confused and guilty.

Rodrigo reports that he experienced those episodes of attempts to repress thoughts and subsequent pleasurable relaxation (when they finally appeared) for several consecutive nights. Finally, one of the nights he voluntarily chose to give up (being unable to avoid the appearance of such thoughts) and masturbated fantasizing about the pony. Rodrigo describes that episode as an impulsive and sudden act, letting himself be carried away by the accumulated frustration of not being able to make the thoughts related to the animal disappear from his mind. According to him, he gave in to temptation so as not to continue suffering.

From there, the more the client tried to control sexual thoughts related to animals, the more intense they became and did not go away until he surrendered to them again by integrating them into a sexual fantasy while masturbating. In addition, Rodrigo mentions that, although he continued to feel attraction to women, gradually his sexual fantasies with the pony became predominant. If Rodrigo started masturbating fantasizing about girls (or about actresses, models, etc. that appeared on television), he was immediately invaded by images of the pony and, no matter how hard he tried, he could no longer resume the initial fantasies with girls. In addition, once he had already started masturbating by fantasizing about women, the flow of sexual arousal, previously triggered by them, made it later more difficult to suppress the fantasies with the pony once they appeared. This process was repeated over and over again, the client feeling increasingly guilty and losing what little self-esteem he had left.

Rodrigo mentions that he came to sense that his strong attempts at control were making him feel worse and worse and he tried to forget about the issue, downplaying it, saying things to himself such as: «They're just fantasies, it's not that serious either» or «I'm not going to give this much importance». These self-comforting words relieved him momentarily, but immediately he thought that he couldn't forget about something so worrying and that it was his moral duty to control those thoughts and make sure that he really wasn't attracted to animals, and then the whole cycle began again.

Rodrigo recounts that, in later years, with the access to pornography with zoophilic content through the Internet, his obsessions progressively became even more intense. The client began to consume, quite frequently, this type of pornography and began to worry about the possibility that he could practice those acts in real life. Since he had previously masturbated thinking about animals (something that at first he considered morally unacceptable), who could assure him that he would not end up passing from fantasy to reality?

Although, in the short term, Rodrigo experienced a great release of tension when he masturbated in the presence of pornographic videos, immediately afterwards he felt very guilty. Rodrigo felt bad after watching those pornographic videos and masturbating but, although each time he promised himself that this would be the last, he always ended up repeating the behavior.

**Functional analysis of the case**

Analyzing all the information provided by the client Rodrigo, he could be diagnosed by stating that he sufres from sexual paraphilia, more specifically zoophilia. Another alternative diagnosis could be Obsessive Compulsive Disorder with obsessions about zoophilia. That said, from an approach based on Functional Analysis, it should be made clear that psychopathological diagnoses have limited clinical utility, since they do not offer any key at a functional level that can guide us when planning a therapeutic intervention. In order to establish the appropriate treatment, it would be essential to carry out a functional analysis of the behavior-problems with the aim of acting on the relevant variables in this specific case.

The behaviors that Rodrigo pointed out as problematic were recurrent sexual fantasies with animals and the consumption of pornography with related content, in addition to concerns about the possibility of moving from fantasy to reality. From a functional point of view, we can consider that the zoophilic sexual fantasies that occur when the client is about to masturbate are preceded by the following responses:

1) Previous verbal-cognitive response: the client has thoughts of the type «I'm sure I'll fall into temptation again», «I have to avoid thinking about animals», «I have to control myself», «These thoughts give me pleasure, I'm weird», «I'm a

vicius, I have no willpower», «I'm a pervert for thinking about these things», «They are only fantasies, it is not that serious either» y «I'm not going to give this much importance».

2) Previous physiological response: The cognitive or verbal responses indicated in the previous point are accompanied by an unpleasant physiological activation (tension, agitation, anxiety, etc.) and some pre-sexual activation (initiation of penile erection movements).

As can be seen, the thoughts associated with fear, avoidance and guilt trigger a physiological activation that the client experiences as unpleasant. In addition, to this unpleasant physiological activation is added the sexual activation caused by images of sexual content (despite the fact that these images were classified as immoral by the client, they generated a groinal response).

In addition, avoidant thoughts paradoxically made the content they intended to avoid even more present in the subject's mind. In our case, when Rodrigo said to himself: «I have to avoid thinking about *animals*», that statement already contained the content avoided «*animals*». In this context, Rodrigo experienced a certain instantaneous relaxation just when that avoided content appeared in his mind, since if the content that you were worried about appearing had already appeared in your mind, you saved yourself some of the effort necessary to continue repressing or suppressing that content.

That small instantaneous relaxation to which we refer, together with the perception of his own pre-sexual activation, made the client feel even more guilty, since he experienced these phenomena as physically pleasurable despite the fact that they were not morally acceptable to him. In addition, these perceptions led him to anticipate the future pleasure that he could experience if he accepted those thoughts by voluntarily fantasizing about them. Indeed, the client carried out small verification probes, briefly fantasizing about these images and verifying that when they appeared, they did so accompanied by a certain pleasure or relaxation. As the results of his probes were not as desired, the client felt more and more confused and guilty and, under these circumstances, the physiological activation became so unbearable that Rodrigo was forced to voluntarily allow and accept the zoophilic fantasies so that this tension decreases.

In summary, Rodrigo experienced great physiological tension when he tried to control his thoughts and all efforts to avoid these sensations were unsuccessful and paradoxically made him feel worse and worse. He already knew that if he masturbated to those fantasies, he would end up feeling bad and guilty about himself later, but the point was that he was already feeling bad before doing it. Furthermore, due to the paradoxical effects of experiential avoidance described above, there was no effective way to suppress such thoughts.

In short, the responses emitted by the client, upon surrendering and masturbating, allowing fantasies of a zoophilic nature, were the following:

1) Verbal-cognitive response: The client, after struggling unsuccessfully to control and try to eliminate sexual content related to animals from his mind, has the following thought: «I can't stand this anguish, I give up».

2) Locomotor response: The client ends up masturbating.

3) Physiological response: Sudden, pleasurable discharge from previous physiological arousal.

As we can see, the client's behavior would follow a pattern of negative reinforcement (the client manages to eliminate physiological discomfort). The consequences of the responses issued are clear, in the short term the client has discharged the physiological discomfort triggered by the attempts to avoid/control the problem behavior and the sexual tension that would have accumulated, but in the long term negative consequences continue to be triggered (increased guilt, association of pleasure with zoophilic stimuli, deterioration of self-esteem, etc.). These negative consequences will end up predisposing the client to try harder to control his thoughts and feelings the next time he is faced with the possibility of masturbating to zoophilic fantasies or the possibility of having real zoophilic contact.

**Therapeutic treatment of the clinical case based on Acceptance and Commitment Therapy**

Taking into account the previous functional and topographic analysis, the therapeutic intervention was aimed at eliminating the control/avoidance behavior of thoughts and sensations, since the control/avoidance attempt itself was the main factor of the problem (Hayes, Strosahl y Wilson, 1999).

The first step consisted of exonerating the client, since he referred to himself with labels such as «zoophílic», «vicious» or «perverted». It was essential to depathologize their problem, for which, in all sessions, the use of the term *paraphilia, bestiality* or similar was avoided at all costs and, instead, the much less stigmatizing term problem was used. In addition, following this line, in reference to the thoughts that disturbed him, we avoided classifying them as *fantasies*, since this denomination implies a certain component of desire, of «wanting to carry it out», and they were referred to as obsessions and cognitive compulsions, so that the client would be clear about his egodystonic character.

Next, the biography exposed by Rodrigo was reviewed so that he became aware that the precipitating factor of his problem was the fact that, in the past, he had classified as immoral something that, due to his age, could be relatively normal. This fact was none other than the one that made reference to the narrated episode where he considered the possibility of having sex with his pony. In this way, it was explained to him how during childhood and adolescence, it is relatively normal for boys, guided by curiosity and sexual awakening, to get involved in sexual games and exploratory practices of all kinds. Furthermore, in any case, he did not get to materialize his idea, since he ultimately regretted it. It was also explained to him how extravagant sexual thoughts (of all kinds) can occasionally occur in anyone and he was emphasized in differentiating the «context self» from the «contained self» through the «metaphor of the zoo and animals». According to this metaphor, the zoo would be equivalent to the self as context while the different animals would refer to the self as content. The qualities that are attributed to animals (good, bad, nice, unpleasant, fierce, docile, pretty, ugly, etc.) do not have to be generalized to the zoo itself.

Continuing with the development of the therapy, another factor that made the client feel guilty was the fact that, although he classified his thoughts as inmoral and could tell that they displeased or bothered him, from a merely physical or physiological point of view they caused him some sensations that could be perceived as pleasurable (erection, arousal and orgasm). To help Rodrigo to distance himself from such situations, it was explained to him that «the penis does not think» and that any content of a sexual nature, no matter how inmoral or extravagant, could momentarily cause an activation of the genitals or groinal response. In his own personal story, his first reaction was to discard the mental content labeled as inmoral, but his insecure and extremely responsible mind was not satisfied, experiential avoidance kicked in and he continued to worry about the subject, forcing him to be in contact once again and again with the dreaded contents.

Once the client had already detached himself, at least partially, from the excessive guilt that he manifested, in subsequent sessions we sought to encourage «creative hopelessness», carrying out the discussion with him about the purpose and usefulness of the control strategies/avoidance that he had been using up to now, so that he clearly understood that such strategies constituted the main factor in maintaining his behavior-problem. In this sense, one of the reasons that led Rodrigo to try to keep his thoughts and mental images related to animals under control was, apart from the fact that he considered them immoral, the fear of being able to go from fantasy to reality. In this regard, it was explained to him that, no matter how much he tried to make sure, there would always be a real possibility of committing the acts he feared. There would always be a chance, however remote. No matter how hard he tried to make sure, he could never be 100 percent sure. Although this approach initially caused Rodrigo anxiety, it eventually helped him realize how ineffective and counterproductive his attemps at control were.

To help him better understand the functional explanations of his problem, an *ad hoc* elaborate metaphor was used, although partly inspired by those previously proposed by Hayes, Strosahl y Wilson (1999) and called the «alarm bell metaphor». According to this metaphor, the unpleasant physiological activation that occurs when contacting the feared mental content would be equivalent to multiple alarms that sound shrilly when there is some danger. Although they may seem useful, since they warn us of the proximity of a danger (in this case masturbation with an immoral mental content), they become unbearable if they are not deactivated in time. The point is that they are programmed to deactivate themselves and any external attempt to turn them off in any other way will make the sound even more shrill.

In this phase of the intervention there was a stagnation , since, despite the fact that the client perfectly understood that the attempts to repress the thoughts he feared caused his physiological activation to increase, he presented great resistance to remaining passive in the face of them, since he was convinced that it was his duty to suppress them. The client had even more difficulty not paying attention to such thoughts when they appeared once he had already started masturbation, since he valued the therapeutic acceptance of the thoughts or images as the generator of his sexual arousal. In this way, Rodrigo did not appreciate any qualitative difference between the therapeutic acceptance that was proposed to him and the surrender that he carried out before his thoughts (what he understood to be fantasizing) before starting the psychological treatment.

In order for the client to assimilate the qualitative differences between both processes (therapeutic acceptance versus compulsive surrender), a new metaphor was used: «the metaphor of the warlike conflict». According to this metaphor, when a war conflict arises, it is not the same for a certain country to declare itself neutral (that is, not to participate in the war) or for the same country to surrender to its enemy or ally with it. In this way, the client, by accepting the intrusive zoophilic thoughts, would be adopting a neutral position, of not participating in his particular war, but in no case of surrender or alliance with that mental content.

Finally, the client committed to accepting that these thoughts would continue to appear and that «the alarm bells» would continue to sound, but that would not be an impediment to carrying out a full life according to his values. In this regard, Rodrigo established finding a girlfriend (this, more than a value, would be more of a goal or objective, but it served from a therapeutic point of view), being   hard-working person, and being a more dynamic and sociable person.

In total, 12 weekly sessions were held, of which one was for the evaluation and presentation of the singularities of ACT and the rest of the sessions were for treatment. After three months, the client was contacted by telephone to follow up on his therapeutic evolution. Rodrigo mentioned that, although he still had sexual thoughts and images related to animals, these were less vivid, were not accompanied by as unpleasant a physiological arousal as he had experienced in the past, and were generally replaced without experiencing guilt. The last telephone contact with the client took place ten months later and served to confirm his positive evolution, since, as he commented, thoughts related to animals hardly appeared and when they did not alter him too much. In relation to his values, although the client had not been able to establish any affective or sexual relationship with women, he was quite optimistic in this regard, assuring that he felt less shy when talking to them and that he had made some friends among his co-workers at the mall.

## CLINICAL CASE 3

## Description of the clinical case

The client in the third clinical case included in this book is Enrique, an 18 year old man who sought help in anguish because he had doubts and obsessive thoughts about his sexual orientation.

Enrique told his story from when he was little, saying that he was the only son in the family and that he had four sisters, three older and one younger than him. Enrique mentioned that he spent a lot of time with them and enjoyed playing typically feminine games such as dolls, «little houses», «rope» or «elastic». Enrique remembers that his parents often scolded him for playing girls'games, warning him that he would become a «fag».

On the other hand, Enrique remembered that since he was little he was  bad at playing children's games and sports in general and that, for this reason, he received a lot of teasing from his classmates at school. They also laughed at his effeminate gestures (the client himself suggests that he adopted them from his sisters by spending so much time with them). This fact affected Enrique a lot and he increasingly distanced himself from the boys at school and grew up being a shy, insecure and introverted boy.

All these previous circumstances were becoming predisposing factors for the subsequent psychological problem for which Rodrigo would end up asking for help, but a precipitating factor was missing. This precipitating factor came when the client was 13 years old and in the eighth grade of school. According to Enrique, in the natural sciences book there was a topic dedicated to sexual education and one of the chapters dealt with the subject of masturbation. Apparently, in that chapter there was a paragraph that said more or less the following:

*«Masturbation is a healthy act that gives us pleasure and that we can practice alone or with the help of a friends.»*

Enrique, who was already masturbating at that time, after reading that in his science book, had the idea of asking his cousin, who was the same age, to masturbate together. His cousin accepted and they both masturbated each other, stroking each other's penis. Enrique assures that these encounters occurred some five or six times from the age of 13, when they began, until the age of 15 when both decided to end it, considering them immoral and inappropriate.

Enrique stated that, although before those acts with this cousin he experienced sexual attraction exclusively towards girls, as a result of those episodes he began to wonder if perhaps boys could also attract him. According to his own reasoning, since the experience of mutual masturbation with his cousin had been physiologically pleasurable (though psychologically inmoral), perhaps he could    experience pleasure with other individuals of his sex. Since then, Enrique often found himself watching other boys. Apparently, he did that to check and make sure if he was attracted or not. He also had a tendency to compare himself to them, since Enrique was a slightly overweight boy with acne and felt inferior to his schoolmates. Most of his classmates were sporty boys who were beginning to have well-built, athletic musculature. In this way, every time Enrique came across an attractive boy, he would look at him carefully to make sure that he was not aroused by any kind of sexual attraction. The client thought that if he looked at them so often and was able to appreciate their attractiveness, it was because he might be gay or bisexual.

On the other hand, the client reported that when he masturbated thinking about girls, he tried to avoid fortuitous images of men coming into his mind. He said to himself: «Don't think about men while you masturbate» and, precisely, paradoxically, images of men appeared in his mind. Enrique mentioned that, without really understanding the reason, these images were accompained by a certain pleasant relaxation, a fact that caused him great anguish. Similarly, he perceived his own erection under the influence of this mental content. Later, in new episodes, the client experienced a kind of anticipation of pleasure when in contact with the images of men. Enrique then tried to make sure that those mental images were not really pleasant to him, briefly fantasizing about them to see what effect they produced on him. To his bewilderment, he discovered that this approach to the images he intended to avoid was indeed pleasurable. Since the result of his probe was not what he expected, but rather he had actually experienced some pleasure or sexual arousal by fantasizing about the mental content he was trying to repress, Enrique felt increasingly confused and guilty.

This vicious circle was repeated night after night, always following the same script. As he reached adulthood, with doubts and insecurities about himself and his sexuality, Enrique began to worry that he might be able to move from fantasy to reality. In addition, the client reported that he experienced considerable difficulties in interacting sexually with women, since his physique was not, according to him, very attractive and he was shy and insecure. Despite these difficulties, his first sexual relationships were with women, but these relationships were not entirely satisfactory for him. Just like the client in the first clinical case presented in this book, Enrique experienced relationships as a kind of test in which he forced himself to enjoy himself to make sure that he was not really homosexual. Ultimately, what ended up happening was that the fact of not fully enjoying women was for our client worrying evidence of his homosexuality.

**Functional analysis of the case**

Analyzing all the information provided by the client Enrique, it seems clear that we would be dealing with a case of what was formerly called egodystonic homosexuality or, as it is usually diagnosed today, internalized homophobia. Now, from an approach based on Functional Analysis, it should be made clear that this diagnostic name has limited practical usefulness, since it does not offer any key at a functional level that can guide us when programming a clinical intervention. To establish the appropriate treatment, it is essential to carry out the Functional Analysis of the problematic behaviours with the objective of acting on the relevant variables of this specific case.

The responses that Enrique points out as problematic are recurring sexual fantasies with men and the possibility of going from fantasy to reality.

From a topographical point of view, we can consider that homosexual fantasies that occur when the client is about to masturbate (stimulating triggering situation) are preceded by the following responses:

1) Previous verbal-cognitive response: The client has the following thought: «I'm sure I'll think about the same thing again», «I have to avoid thinking about men», «Deep down, these thoughts give me pleasure, maybe I like men», «I'm abnormal for thinking these things».

2) Previous physiological response: Unpleasant physiological activation (tension, agitation, anxiety, etc.) and certain pre-sexual activation (beginning of penile erection movements).

As can be seen, thoughts related to fear, avoidance and guilt are accompanied by a physiological activation that the client experiences as aversive. Furthermore, this unpleasant physiological activation is joined by sexual activation caused by images of sexual content (despite being classified as inmoral and inappropriate by the client).

On the other hand, avoidant thoughts paradoxically make the contents that are intended to be avoided become even more present in the client (Hayes, Wilson, Gifford, Follette & Stroshal, 1996). In our case, when Enrique says to himself: «I have to avoid thinking about *men*», that statement already contains the avoided content «*men*». The client experiences some instant relaxation just when that avoided content appears in his mind: «*men*», since if the content that he was worried about appearing has already appeared in his mind, he saves himself some of the effort necessary to continue repressing or suppressing that content.

This small fortuitous relaxation combined with the perception of his own pre-sexual activation makes the client feel even more guilty, since he values these experiences as physically pleasurable even though they do not sem. morally acceptable. Additionally, these perceptions focus him on anticipating the future pleasure he may experience if he accepts those thoughts or mental images voluntarily, rather than attempering to repress them. Therefore, the client decides to carry out small «experiments» or test probes, briefly fantasizing about those thoughts or mental images, to check if they really are pleasurable or not. Indeed, when the client allows this mental content to appear, he experiences pleasure by releasing the unpleasant physiological activation caused by the repression efforts. Because the results of his surveys are not as desired, the client feels increasingly confused and guilty.

The client experienced great physiological tension when he tried to control or avoid his thoughts and sensations and all his efforts were fruitless paradoxically caused him to feel worse and worse. He already knew that if he masturbated to these fantasies, he would end up feeling bad and guilty about himself later, but the thing is that he was already feeling bad before he did it and, furthermore, due to the paradoxical effects of experiential avoidance described above, he would not there was an effective way to suppress such thoughts and sensations.

The responses that the client emits, when he surrenders and masturbates, allowing homosexual fantasies, are  the following:

1) Verbal-cognitive response: The client, after struggling unsuccessfully to control and try to eliminate sexual content related to men, has the following thought: «I can't stand this anguish, I give up».

2) Locomotor response: The client ends up masturbating.

3) Physiological response: Sudden, pleasurable discharge from previous physiological arousal.

As we see, the client's behavior, as occurred with that of the clients in the clinical cases explained above, would follow a pattern of negative reinforcement (the client manages to eliminate physiological discomfort). The consequences of the responses issued are clear: in the short term the client has discharged the physiological discomfort triggered by the attemps to control the problem behavior, but in the long term negative consequences continue to be triggered (increased guilt, increased morality conflict by associating pleasure with homosexual stimuli, deterioration of the subject's self-esteem, etc.). These negative consequences will predispose the client to try harder to control his thoughts and sensations the next time he is faced with the possibility of masturbating to homosexual fantasies or the possibility of having authentic homosexual contact.

**Therapeutic treatment of the clinical case based on Acceptance and Commitment Therapy**

Taking into account the previous functional analysis, the clinical intervention was aimed at making the client rethink the functionality of his behavior of control or avoidance of thoughts and sensations, given that the attempt at control or avoidance itself constituted the  main factor of his problem.

.      The first step was to encourage «creative hopelessness» (Wilson y Luciano, 2002) so that the client became aware that, despite all his efforts to control or avoid the thoughts or sensations that tormented him, he had not achieved any positive results. To facilitate this process, the «metaphor of water and the strainer» was used. As a summary, this metaphor exposes the situation of a man who tries to cover the holes of a strainer with his fingers to prevent water from spilling through them. The result is that for every hole that manages to plug, there is another that remains free and the water continues to spill.

Although the client perfectly understood that attempts to repress the thoughts he feared caused his physiological arousal to increase, he had great resistance to remaining passive in the face of them, because he was convinced that it was his duty to suppress them. At this point in the intervention, we sought to promote the process known as «separation of the context self and the content self». For this, it was explained to the client how, regardless of one´s sexual orientation, it is normal for people to occasionally have sexual thoughts of diverse content and that this does not imply that one necessarily agrees with those contents or that he wants to put the situations they represent into practice in real life. Two metaphors that were used in this phase of the treatment, among several others that are not presented here for reasons of space, were «the house and the furniture» and «the board and the piece» (Wilson y Luciano, 2002). According to these metaphors, the house and the board are equivalent to the context self, while furniture and piece are equivalent to the content self. The qualities attributed to the furniture or the pieces (good, bad, pleasant, unpleasant, appropiate, inappropiate, moral, inmoral, etc.) do not have to be generalized to the house or the board.

As occurred in the two clinical cases described above, one of the reasons that led Enrique to try to keep sexual thoughts and mental images related to men under control was, apart from the fact that he considered them inmoral, fear to be able to go from fantasy to reality. In this regard, it was explained to him that, no matter how much he tried to ensure himself, there would always be a real possibility of committing the acts he feared. There would always be a possibility, no matter how remote. No matter how much he tried to make sure, he could never be one hundred percent sure. Although this approach generated some anxiety for the client, several work sessions were carried out to expose their thoughts through the experiential exposure exercise that appears in the manual by Wilson and Luciano (2002). The client experienced a reduction in anxiety associated with these cognitions of uncertainty about the future and ultimately realized how ineffective and counterproductive his attempts at control were.

Finally, Enrique committed to accepting that his thoughts would continue to appear, but that would not be an impediment to leading a full life according to his values, aimed at achieving goals. In this regard, the client established the values of being a hard-working person, being a less shy person, and being a brave person. To finish the intervention with Enrique, several sessions were dedicated to training in social skills using the modeling technique and the role-playing.

In total, 14 weekly sessions were carried out, of which two were evaluation and 12 were treatment. After two months, the client was contacted by telephone to monitor his therapeutic evolution. Enrique reported that, although he still had thoughts and images related to men, were not accompanied by such unpleasant physiological arousal as he had experienced in the past, and were usually replaced without too much difficulty by fantasies related to women. Six months later, the last telephone contact with Enrique was made and his positive evolution was confirmed, since, according to the client, thoughts related to men barely appeared and when they did they did not alter him too much, even if they appeared during the masturbation in the phases of maximum excitement. In relation to his values, the client had gotten a job as a warehouse boy in a supermarket and, although he had not managed to start any heterosexual romantic relationship, he stated that he had met quite a few girls and felt less shy and much more confident and comfortable when interacting socially with them.

## GENERAL CONCLUSIONS

Assuming the need for more empirical validation to support the effectiveness of ACT in the treatment of sexual obsessions, the results obtained in each of the cases presented allow us to harbor a certain optimism about the possibilities of this form of therapy. ACT must be taken into account when addressing psychological problems where the experiential avoidance of private events (thoughts, emotions, bodily sensations, etc.) constitutes a determining element as a factor in maintaining said problems.

As has been seen throughout the clinical cases analyzed in this book, all three share the same explanation at a functional level, sharing as a key factor the experiential avoidance of different private events. Although two cases presented obsessions related to people of the same sex, while another presented sexual obsessions related to animals, therefore different in terms of content, functionally they are not only similar, but the three are practically identical, clones. That is why, being three very different people, their therapeutic journey was surprisingly similar, as we could say, as was the final result of the treatment.

The techniques used in ACT allow individuals to become clearly aware of the paradoxical and counterproductive phenomena of experiential avoidance and help them break the vicious circles in which they find themselves immersed with no way out, circles that are very characteristic of problems of sexual obsessions.

Regarding the prevention of the psychological problems analyzed in this book, the predisposing factors that would favor the appearance of Experiential Avoidance Disorder would be the contexts of fusion/literality, giving reasons, evaluation/valuation and control/avoidance, contexts, all of them, socially reinforced. These contexts promote pathological fusion with one´s own private events (fusion/literality), the search for a cause or explanation for those private events (giving reasons), their constant analysis (evaluation/valuation) and attempts to eliminate, or at least keep under control private events that are valued as aversive (control/avoidance). In this way, it is considered essential to mention the importance of preventing avoidance patterns from childhood, since these are at the basis of the clinical problems addressed in this book. The more contexts of fusion, evaluation, avoidance and reason-giving are encouraged, the more insecure people will be and the more they will strive to keep their private events  such as thoughts, physiological sensations, mental images or emotions under control.

Finally, before finishing, I consider it vitally important to make a clarification. I do not consider homosexuality as something unnatural or inusual, since it arises in nature itself and, in fact, in addition to human beings, it frequently appears in many animal species. Therefore, I would like to make it clear that, with the application of ACT in the cases of Sandra and Enrique, I did not «heal» their homosexuality. A homosexual orientation is not a disease. Adult homosexuals who are happy carrying out homosexual practices deserve all my respect and tolerate and can live their lives as they see fit, nothing more. Although in the past, homosexuals were considered psychiatric patients and subjecting to various conversion therapies (some as cruel as subjecting people to electric shocks while they looked at images of individuals of their sex) to turn them heterosexual, in recent years these therapies have been banned in many countries. A psychologist or psychiatrist who continues to carry out conversion therapies is exposed to heavy financial penalties or even the withdrawal of his or her professional title. Therefore, I would like to make it clear that I do not do conversion therapies and that Sandra and Enrique's clinical cases are not, in any case, covert or masked conversion therapies. I only treat a series of obsessions (which in those cases in question were of a sexual nature), in the same way that OCD obsessions are treated. Just in case, I'm going to repeat it once again, I do not «cure» homosexuality. On a legal, theoretical and practical level there is a big difference between carrying out conversion therapy to make a homosexual or bisexual person become heterosexual and getting someone with sexual obsessions or internalized homophobia to stop being tormented by their thoughts. In the clinical cases described, the therapeutic objective was not in any case to eliminate thoughts related to homosexuality, but rather for the clients to lead a valuable life in the direction of their personal values despite these thoughts (the decrease in such thoughts was a secondary result). In ACT the goal is never the reduction of symptoms but rather for clients to continue functioning toward their values despite those symptoms. Under this approach is how the clinical cases presented in this book were approached. If during the subsequent post-treatment follow-up phase, both Sandra and Enrique had reported that they had had real sexual contacts with people of the same sex, the therapy would have been considered equally successful as long as both continued walking in the direction of their values.

People are different, their thoughts and emotions are also different. Therefore, I would like to propose two alternative treatment routes, depending on each case:

1ª) The intervention aimed at the full liberation of repressed homosexuality. This intervention would only be possible in some cases of egodystonic homosexuality or bisexuality, in which the patient, now an adult, has made the determination to accept the homosexual or bisexual tendency, discarding the exclusively heterosexual orientation. It is usually the best option in cases where the client has gone from fantasies to reality and has already had homosexual contacts with other people. In this cases, any form of therapy intended to direct him toward heterosexuality could be considered conversion therapy, which would likely cause unnecessary suffering and be ineffective.

2ª) The intervention aimed at breaking the vicious circles in which the subjects have become immersed. This intervention would imply the acceptance of mental contents related to homosexuality as if they were any other type of obsessions. It would be the ideal intervention for adolescent or young adult clients who have doubts or insecurities about their sexuality but who continue to feel attraction to people of the opposite sex and a strong resistance to carrying out real homosexual behaviors. In these cases, it is essential that the subject understands that his attempts to expel the avoided content from his mind paradoxically produce an increase in its intensity. To achieve this, the ACT that I used in the cases of Sandra and Enrique is an effective tool.

www.ingramcontent.com/pod-product-compliance
Lightning Source LLC
Chambersburg PA
CBHW070957250726
48663CB00002B/271